Examining Evidence
for God's Existence

by Phil Fernandes

Does God Exist?
by Dr. Phil Fernandes

Printed in the United States of America

ISBN-13: 978-1723493379
ISBN-10: 1723493376

IBD Press
P. O. Box 3264
Bremerton, WA 98310
www.philfernandes.com

Dedication

This book is dedicated to:

my wife Cathy

and

my former professor and mentor Dr. Norman Geisler

About the Author

Dr. Phil Fernandes is the senior pastor of Trinity Bible Fellowship and the president of the Institute of Biblical Defense. Fernandes teaches apologetics, philosophy, and ethics at Crosspoint Academy, Veritas International University, Columbia Evangelical Seminary, and Shepherds Bible College. He has earned a Ph.D. in philosophy of religion from Greenwich University, a Doctor of Theological Studies from Columbia Evangelical Seminary, and a Master of Arts in Religion from Liberty University. Fernandes is completing work on a Doctor of Ministry in Apologetics Degree through Southern Evangelical Seminary. He is a member of the following professional societies: The Evangelical Theological Society, the Society of Christian Philosophers, the Evangelical Philosophical Society, and the International Society of Christian Apologetics. Dr. Fernandes has publicly debated some of America's leading atheists at schools such as Princeton University and the University of North Carolina at Chapel Hill. He has authored several books dealing with the defense of the Christian faith. Hundreds of Dr. Fernandes' lectures, debates, and sermons can be downloaded from his websites: www.philfernandes.com and www.instituteofbiblicaldefense.com.

Books Authored or Co-Authored by Phil Fernandes:

The God Who Sits Enthroned: Evidence for God's Existence
(Xulon Press, 2002)

No Other Gods: A Defense of Biblical Christianity
(Xulon Press, 2002)

God, Government, and the Road to Tyranny:
A Christian View of Government and Morality
(Xulon Press, 2003; co-authored with Eric Purcell, Kurt Rinear, and
Rorri Wiesinger)

Decay of a Nation: The Need for National Revival
(Triune Press, 1987-no longer in print)

Theism versus Atheism: The Internet Debate
(IBD Press, 1997, 2000; co-authored with Dr. Michael Martin)

Contend Earnestly for the Faith: A Survey of Christian Apologetics
(Publish America, 2007)

The Atheist Delusion: A Christian Response to Christopher Hitchens
and Richard Dawkins
(Xulon Press, 2009)

Evidence for Faith: Essays in Christian Apologetics
(IBD Press, 2009: co-authored with Gary Tronson and Erik Stenerson)

Seven Great Apologists: Seven Defenders of the Faith Who Impacted
Their World
(IBD Press, 2011)

Hijacking the Historical Jesus: Answering Recent Attacks on the Jesus of the Bible
(IBD Press, 2012; co-authored with Kyle Larson)

Is Hell Forever? Does the Bible Teach That Hell will be Annihilation or Eternal Torment?
(co-authored with Chris Date)

The Fernandes Guide to Apologetic Methodologies
(IBD Press, 2016)

Vital Issues in the Inerrancy Debate
(Wipf and Stock, 2015; co-authored with David Farnell, Norman Geisler, Joe Holden, and Bill Roach)

Dr. Fernandes also contributed to the following books:

The Big Argument: Does God Exist? Twenty-Four Scholars Explore How Science, Archaeology, and Philosophy Haven't Disproved God
(Master Books, 2006; edited by John Ashton and Michael Westacott)

Harvest Handbook on Christian Apologetics
(Harvest House Publishers, 2018; edited by Joseph Holden)

Introduction
Atheism and Agnosticism

Does God exist? Is there evidence for His existence? If God does exist, is He a personal God or a non-personal force? What is God like? This booklet will attempt to answer these questions and provide evidence for the existence of a personal God (i.e., theism).

Atheism is the belief that it can be proven that God does not exist.[1] Agnosticism, on the other hand, is the belief that man cannot know whether or not God exists.[2] It is possible to hold weaker forms of either view.[3] However, this booklet is only concerned with refuting the more dogmatic forms of atheism and agnosticism. Only the stronger forms, if proven, would defeat theism (the belief in a personal, Creator God). The weaker forms leave open the possibility of theism. However, both atheism and agnosticism, in their strongest forms, are self-refuting.

In order for one to disprove God's existence (atheism), he would have to be all-knowing.[4] One would need to have the ability to see and

---

[1]Norman Geisler and Paul Feinberg, *Introduction to Philosophy* (Grand Rapids: Baker Book House, 1980), 430.

[2]Ibid., 429.

[3]Ibid., 296.

1

know all things in the physical and spiritual realms. In short, one would have to be God to disprove God's existence. Of course, this is absurd.

Agnosticism is also self-defeating. One must know something about God to know that nothing can be known about God.[5] Obviously, this statement refutes itself. Therefore, agnosticism, like atheism, is a self-refuting view.

Many agnostics say that since man is finite (limited), he can never attain knowledge of an infinite (unlimited) Being. It is true that the finite cannot find the infinite on its own. However, this ignores the possibility that the infinite Being may choose to reveal Himself to finite beings. This is exactly what Christianity claims. The Bible teaches that God reveals Himself through both nature (Rom. 1:18-22; Ps. 19:1) and the scriptures (2 Tim. 3:16-17; 2 Pet. 1:20-21).

---

[4]Norman Geisler, *Christian Apologetics* (Grand Rapids; Baker Book House, 1976), 233.

[5]Geisler and Feinberg, 298-299.

Chapter One
The Failure of Atheism

Does God exist? And, if He does exist, is there evidence for His existence? This booklet will attempt to answer these questions. First, it will be shown that atheism (i.e., the belief there is no God) has failed as a world view (a way to explain reality).

Did Man Invent God?

Throughout history several atheist thinkers have proclaimed their belief that God was a product of man's imagination. Ludwig Feuerbach (1804-1872) taught that man, due to his fear of death, wishes God into existence. Man recognizes his limitations and fears. God is projected to calm these fears. In short, God is what man wishes to be.[6]

Sigmund Freud (1856-1939) saw two separate causes for man's belief in God. First, Freud believed that boys sexually desire their mothers. Because of this, he becomes jealous of his father and develops a hatred for him. Second, since man could not fully understand the forces of nature, he began to fear nature. Freud concluded that due to

---

[6]William S. Sahakian, *History of Philosophy* (New York: Harper Collins Publishers, 1968), 202.

3

these two factors (man's guilt for hating his father and man's fear of nature), mankind deified nature and personalized it into a Father God.[7]

It should be understood that the speculations of Feuerbach and Freud were never meant to be used as arguments against God's existence. Instead, these two thinkers believed that God's existence had already been proven false by the advances of modern science. Their views were promoted not to disprove God's existence. Rather, they were promoted as a desperate attempt to explain why nearly all of mankind believes in a non-existent God. Therefore, the ideas of Feuerbach and Freud should not be considered evidence against God's existence. Instead, their theories were merely attempts to explain away some of the evidence against their views.[8]

Freud's own theories can be used against him. For it seems more likely that *atheism* is caused by the desire to kill the father image, rather than theism being caused by man's guilt for wanting to kill his father.[9] In man's attempt to be autonomous, he wishes God out of existence.

Whatever the case, the speculations of Feuerbach and Freud seem to be wishful thinking by atheists. If men were to invent a God, it is doubtful that it would be the demanding God of the Bible.[10] Man would create a more permissive god, much like the gods of the pagan religions. In short, the theories of Feuerbach and Freud offer a more adequate explanation for atheism and idolatry than they do for Christianity.[11]

---

[7]Sigmund Freud, *The Future of an Illusion*, trans. W. D. Robson-Scott (New York: Doubleday, 1964), 20-27.

[8]R. C. Sproul, *If There's a God, Why are there Atheists?* (Wheaton: Tyndale House Publishers, 1978), 49-50.

[9]J. P. Moreland, *Scaling the Secular City* (Grand Rapids: Baker Book House, 1987), 229.

[10]Sproul, 58, 145-146.

[11]Ibid.

A. J. Ayer and Logical Positivism

In the first half of this century, A. J. Ayer and his colleagues popularized their view of logical positivism. Logical positivism was based upon the verification principle. This principle stated that for a statement to be meaningful, it has to be either true by definition or verifiable by one or more of the five senses.[12] This meant that all discussion about God should be considered meaningless.[13]

If true, this view would be very damaging for theism. Though it would not prove God's nonexistence, it would make all talk about God meaningless.[14] If one cannot meaningfully talk about God, one cannot speculate about his possible existence.

However, the problem with the verification principle is that it is itself not true by definition or verifiable by one or more of the five senses.[15] In other words, the verification principle is self-refuting. If the verification principle is true, then it is itself meaningless, for it fails its own test.[16]

If atheism is to deliver a fatal blow to theism, it will have to look elsewhere. Logical positivism has failed to render discussion about God meaningless.

Is Talk about God Equivocal or Incoherent?

Some have maintained that all talk about God is equivocal.[17] In other words, they believe that terms used to describe God have totally

---

[12]Norman Geisler and Paul Feinberg, 50.

[13]Ibid.

[14]Ibid.

[15]Ibid.

[16]Ibid.

[17]Geisler and Corduan, *Philosophy of Religion* (Grand Rapids: Baker Book House, 1988), 252-271.

different meanings than when they are used in connection with finite beings such as man. If this is true, then man cannot know anything about God. If someone says God is holy, he has uttered a meaningless statement. For man knows what holiness means only when it refers to a man. Man has no idea of what holiness means when applied to God. What holiness means in reference to an infinite being (God) cannot be known by finite beings. If the theist is justified in his or her claims to know something about God, then this objection must be answered.

Some theists have argued that terms used to describe God are univocal.[18] This means that they have totally the same meaning when used to describe both God and man. The problem with this view is that it is hard to believe that God is holy in the same way that man can be holy. For God is infinitely holy, whereas man is only finitely holy. Can holiness have the exact meaning for both man and God? Obviously not.

Other theists contend that religious language is analogical.[19] They hold that terms used of God and man are not equivocal (totally different meanings) or univocal (totally the same meanings). Instead, terms used of God and man are only analogical (similar meanings). However, this view is also problematic. For if God-talk is analogical, then theologians are still using meaningless terms about God. For terms like "holiness" still lack the same meaning they hold when used of men. We can only know what holiness means when it is applied to man. It appears that there must be some univocal element to God-talk if it is to be meaningful.[20]

The answer to this dilemma comes from Thomas Aquinas. He reasoned that words have the same meaning (univocal) when applied to either God or man. However, Aquinas taught that they can only be applied in a similar (analogical) way.[21] Therefore, holiness means the

---

[18]Ibid., 252.

[19]Ibid., 253.

[20]Ibid., 255.

same thing for both man and God. Still, it must be applied finitely to man and infinitely to God. Therefore, God-talk is not equivocal. Theists can meaningfully talk about God.

Jean-Paul Sartre

Jean-Paul Sartre was a famous French philosopher and atheist. He argued that if the theist persists in his assertion that everything needs a cause, then even God needs a cause. Therefore, the theist, according to Sartre, must argue that God caused His own existence. But, this would make God a self-caused being, which is impossible.[22] For a being to cause its own existence, it must exist before it existed in order to bring itself into existence. However, it is absurd to say that a being existed before it existed. Therefore, reasoned Sartre, since God is a self-caused being, He cannot exist.

However, no informed theist believes that everything (including God) needs a cause. Only dependent beings (beings that have a beginning) need a cause. Since God is an independent and eternal being, He does not need a cause.[23] God is not a self-caused being. He is an uncaused being. His existence needs no cause for He always existed.

Sartre also contended that since man is free, God cannot exist. In his view, if man is free (and Sartre believed so), then there could be no sovereign God. If a sovereign God exists, then men are robots.[24]

There have been two ways that theists respond to this argument. One can take a hyper-Calvinistic position and deny human free will.[25] Or, one can simply maintain that God sovereignly chose to make man free.[26]

---

[21]Ibid., 263-264.

[22]Geisler and Feinberg, 293.

[23]Ibid.

[24]Ibid., 295.

[25]Ibid.

Still, man is not absolutely free. He is free to disobey God and reject Christ, but he is not free to escape the God-ordained consequences of his actions. In short, neither of Sartre's objections presents insurmountable problems for theism.

Bertrand Russell

The great British philosopher and mathematician Bertrand Russell reasoned that if everything needs a cause, then so does God. But if God doesn't need a cause, then neither does the universe.[27] As mentioned above, the theist responds to this by pointing out that not everything needs a cause. Only that which has a beginning needs a cause. Since God does not have a beginning, He needs no cause.[28]

Secondly, there is both scientific and philosophical evidence that the universe had a beginning. Scientific evidence consists in the second law of thermodynamics (energy deterioration) and the big bang model. The second law of thermodynamics shows that the amount of usable energy in the universe is running down. Therefore, the universe will eventually cease to exist when all its energy is used up. But if the universe will have an end, it had to have a beginning. This means that the universe began with all its energy in a usable state. Hence, the universe had a beginning.[29]

The big bang model reveals that the universe is expanding at an equal rate in all directions. This is much like the effects of an explosion which blows debris in all directions. If one goes back in time, the universe would become more and more dense until the entire universe

---

[26]Ibid.

[27]Bertrand Russell, *Why I am not a Christian* (New York: Touchstone Books, 1957), 6-7.

[28]Geisler and Feinberg, 293.

[29] Roy E. Peacock, *A Brief History of Eternity* (Wheaton: Crossway Books, 1990), 67-69.

would be compressed into an infinitely small point. This would mark the beginning of the universe.[30]

The scientific evidence for the beginning of the universe does not stand alone. Philosophical evidence can be found as well. For if the universe is eternal, there would be an infinite amount of actual events in the past. But then it would be impossible to reach the present moment. For no matter how many events one traverses, there will always be an infinite amount of events left. Hence, the present moment could never be reached. But the present moment has been reached. This proves that there is only a finite number of events in the past. Therefore, the universe had a first event. In other words, the universe had a beginning.[31]

Bertrand Russell's objection therefore loses its force. The universe cannot be eternal. It must have a cause. Eventually one must arrive at a first cause, a being that needs no cause. This uncaused being is what the theist calls God.

Albert Camus

The French existentialist Albert Camus authored the novel entitled *The Plague*. In this work, Camus argued that if God allowed the plague to occur, then to fight the plague is to fight God. Therefore, to be religious, one must be anti-humanitarian. Only the atheist can be a humanitarian and remain consistent with his beliefs.[32]

Camus' argument has been adequately answered. Even though God permits the plague (symbolic for evil and human suffering) for the purpose of a greater good, He is nonetheless working to defeat the

---

[30]Hugh Ross, *The Creator and the Cosmos* (Colorado Springs: NavPress, 1993), 19-27.

[31]William Lane Craig, *Apologetics, An Introduction* (Chicago: Moody Press, 1984), 81.

[32] Geisler and Corduan, 365.

plague.[33] In fact, the greater good coming from God permitting the plague may include the godly man joining God to battle the plague.[34] Just because God allows something to occur does not make it in itself good. For God could and does allow evil to occur for the purpose of a good that He will bring from the evil.

Therefore, a person can be religious and also be humanitarian without going against his or her beliefs. On the other hand, what is to prevent the atheist from doing whatever he pleases? It seems that the Christian humanitarian is more consistent with his or her beliefs than the atheist is. For in atheism there is no final judgment and moral values are mere human inventions. Atheists are not being consistent with their world view whenever they condemn an action as wrong.

Antony Flew

British philosopher Antony Flew claimed that since there is no way to falsify God's existence, to assert that He does exist is an incoherent statement.[35] Flew is famous for his parable of the invisible gardener.[36] In this parable, a believer and a non-believer come upon a garden in the midst of the wilderness. The believer assumes that there exists a gardener who cares for the garden. The non-believer, however, disagrees. He concludes that there is no gardener. They were not able to detect the existence of the gardener though they ran several tests. They did not see or hear him enter the garden. Even bloodhounds could not smell him. Rather than surrender his faith in the gardener, the believer reasons that the gardener must be invisible and unable to be detected by the five senses. The non-believer responds by stating that there is no

---

[33]Ibid., 365-366.

[34]Ibid.

[35]John Hick, ed. *The Existence of God* (New York: The Macmillian Company, 1964), 224-226.

[36]Ibid.

10

difference between this invisible gardener and no gardener at all. In other words, if there is no way to falsify a view, then the view is worthless.[37]

Flew declares that just as there is no way to falsify the existence of the invisible gardener, so too the existence of the Christian God cannot be falsified. In short, to claim that God exists is to make a meaningless statement. There is no way to prove it false; nothing is allowed to count against it.

In response to Flew's objection, several things can be noted. First, the believer views the universe as dependent and in need of a cause. If there were no independent God, there would also be no dependent universe. If the universe could be shown to exist independent of any cause, then this would go a long way to falsifying the God hypothesis. However, scientific and philosophical arguments for an eternal and independent universe have not been successful. Recent thought seems to lead in the other direction.[38]

Second, the God of the Bible is not a silent God who is unable to be detected. The Judeo-Christian scriptures are filled with prophecies that were fulfilled hundreds of years after they were recorded.[39] If these prophecies had failed, then the God of the Bible would be falsified.

Third, Christianity claims that the God of the Bible has become a man (John 1:1,14). The invisible gardener has taken visible form. Jesus claimed to be God incarnate. Jesus gave persuasive evidence for this claim by performing numerous miracles in the presence of eyewitnesses. His greatest miracle was when He rose from the dead and appeared to many eyewitnesses. If the first century Jewish religious leaders had produced the rotting corpse of Christ, they would have falsified Christ's claims and crushed Christianity in its embryonic form.

---

[37]Ibid.

[38]Craig, 73-95.

[39]Henry M. Morris, *Many Infallible Proofs* (El Cajon: Master Books, 1974), 181-199.

Despite the fact that the Jewish religious leaders had the desire to do so, they did not produce the body.

What needs to be noted here is that the belief in the existence of the God of the Bible is open to testing and falsification. Instead of claiming that God is an incoherent concept incapable of being falsified, Flew would do better to examine the evidence for the Christian God and then attempt to prove as false the claim that He exists. In fact, although he was considered by many to be the world's leading philosophical atheist, Flew eventually became convinced by the evidence that God did in fact exist.[40]

Arguments from Contradictory Attributes

One attempt to refute the existence of God is to claim that the God of the Bible has certain characteristics that are contradictory.[41] If this can be proven, the Christian God cannot exist. This atheistic endeavor can take its form in several different arguments. Two examples will suffice.

Atheists often argue that if God is all-powerful, then He can do anything. This would include the ability to create a rock so large that even He cannot lift it. But if God cannot lift this rock, He is not all-powerful. Therefore, concludes the atheist, no all-powerful God can exist.[42]

Though the theist agrees that God is all-powerful, he recognizes that there are some things that even an all-powerful being cannot do. Since an all-powerful being will always be able to accomplish whatever He sets out to do, it is impossible for an all-powerful being to fail. The above atheistic argument is arguing that since God is all-powerful He

---

[40]Antony Flew, *There is a God: How the World's Most Notorious Atheist Changed His Mind* (New York: Harper Collins, 2007).

[41]Geisler and Feinberg, 294.

[42]Ibid., 294-295.

can do anything, even fail. This is like saying that since God is all-powerful He can be not all-powerful. Obviously, this is absurd. An all-powerful being cannot fail. Therefore, God can create a rock of tremendous size, but, since He is all-powerful, He will always be able to lift it.[43]

There are several things that an all-powerful being cannot do: He cannot lie, sin, or change His mind (Numbers 23:19; James 1:13; 1 Samuel 15:29). Anything that indicates failure cannot be attributed to God.[44]

It should also be noted that God cannot do whatever is impossible by definition. For instance, God cannot create square circles.[45] He cannot create a human that is non-human. He cannot make something both exist and not exist at the same time.

In short, when one says that God is all-powerful, one means that God is able to accomplish all that He desires to do. It means that God can do everything that is possible.[46] But even an all-powerful being cannot do what is impossible by definition. God can do many things that are humanly impossible. However, there are some things that even an all-powerful being cannot do.

Therefore, since God is all-powerful, He will always be able to master His creation. He will always be able to lift any rock that He creates. And, since all that exists (besides Himself) is His creation, there is no rock, nor will there ever be a rock, that He cannot lift.

A second example of an argument against God from supposed contradictory attributes is as follows. If something is good simply because God wills it, then good is merely an arbitrary concept. But, if

---

[43] Ibid., 273-274.

[44] Geisler, *Apologetics*, 229.
[45] Ibid.

[46] Ibid.

God wills it because it is good, then good is a standard above God. Therefore, either good is arbitrary or good is above God.[47]

If the theist concedes either of these two propositions, the concept of God will be damaged. For if good is arbitrary, then calling God good says nothing more than He does what He wills to do. He doesn't do what is right. He simply acts arbitrarily. Whatever He does automatically is considered right for the mere reason that it is an act of God.

If the theist takes the other alternative of the dilemma, the situation is no better. For if God decides to do something because it is good, it appears that there is a standard of right and wrong above God. But then God would not be the ultimate being. A necessary element of the traditional Christian concept of God is that He is the ultimate being. There is no being greater than God (not even goodness). However, God cannot be the ultimate being if there is a standard of right and wrong to which He must submit. The standard itself would be the ultimate being since it would be above God.

Those who use this objection against theism fail to acknowledge that God wills something because it is consistent with His own good nature. Therefore, the standard is not above God; God is the standard.[48] Thus, good is not arbitrary, for it is based upon God's good nature.[49]

The Problem of Evil

Many atheists believe that the existence of evil is proof that an all-good and all-powerful God does not exist.[50] The problem of evil will be dealt with, in detail, after the case for the theistic God has been made.

---

[47]Geisler and Feinberg, 226.

[48]Ibid.

[49]Ibid.

[50]Geisler and Corduan, 295-385.

Chapter Two: The Failure of Other Non-Theistic World Views

Theism is the view of reality which holds to the existence of a personal God who is separate (transcendent) from the universe though involved (immanent) with it.[51] Theists believe that there is one true personal Creator God who can intervene in the affairs of man by performing miracles. Christianity, Judaism, and Islam are the three main theistic religions.[52]

It has been shown that atheism, the world view that there is no God, has failed to prove its case. This means that theism may be true. It is therefore possible that God exists. However, before looking into arguments for the existence of the theistic God, discussion of other non-theistic world views is necessary to show that they have also failed to prove their cases.

The non-theistic world views (other than atheism) include pantheism, panentheism, deism, finite theism, and polytheism. If these world views fail as atheism has failed, then the case for theism will become more probable since it is the only remaining major world view.

---

[51]Norman L. Geisler and William D. Watkins, *Worlds Apart* (Grand Rapids: Baker Book House, 1984), 38.

[52]Geisler, *Apologetics*, 263.

Of course, the case for theism will reach a high degree of probability only if strong arguments can be advanced in its favor.

Pantheism: God is the Universe

Pantheism is the world view that teaches that God is the universe.[53] Pantheism is based upon monism, the belief that all reality is one being.[54] Hinduism and some adherents of Buddhism are pantheistic in their thought.[55] The New Age Movement (the invasion of Western Society with Hindu thought) is also pantheistic.[56]

Pantheism teaches that God is not a personal being. Instead, God is an impersonal force.[57] Since pantheists believe that all reality is one being and that God is this one reality, they believe that each individual is God.[58] In fact, individual existence is merely an illusion since all reality is one being.[59]

There are several problems for pantheism which cause it to fail as a world view. First, many beings exist, not just one.[60] As Christian philosopher Norman Geisler has pointed out, it is actually undeniable that I exist.[61] For if I attempt to deny my existence, I must first exist to

---

[53]Geisler and Watkins, 98-99.

[54]Geisler, *Apologetics*, 173-174.

[55]Geisler and Watkins, 78-79.

[56]Ibid., 94.

[57]Ibid., 98.

[58]Ibid., 96.

[59]Ibid., 99.

[60]Geisler, *Apologetics*, 187.

[61]Ibid., 239.

make the denial.[62] For nothing can deny nothing. Only an existent being can deny its own existence. Therefore, I exist. However, if I try to convince others that I alone exist, I must first affirm their own individual and separate existence by communicating with them.[63] In other words, to argue for pantheism is to admit that pantheism is false. To argue with others is to affirm the existence of others, and if more than one being exists, then pantheism cannot be true.

A second problem with pantheism is that there is strong evidence that the universe had a beginning. Both the big bang model and the second law of thermodynamics reveal this.[64] Also, if the universe is eternal, the present moment could never have arrived. But since the present moment has arrived, only a finite number of events could have occurred in the past.[65] Therefore, there was a first event. The universe had a beginning. Since from nothing, nothing comes, everything that had a beginning needs a cause. Hence, the universe needs a cause.[66] But, for pantheism to be true, the universe would have to be eternal and uncaused.

Third, pantheism claims that reality is ultimately impersonal. This is the same as saying that reality is non-intelligent and non-moral.[67] But for someone to deny the reality of intelligence, he must first assume he has the intelligence to make the denial.[68] Even pantheists pass moral judgments on others. In fact, many pantheists have been known to

---

[62]Ibid.

[63]Ibid., 241.

[64]Craig, 81-93.

[65]Ibid., 81.

[66]Ibid., 93.

[67]Geisler, *Apologetics*, 247-249.

[68]Ibid., 247-248.

protest violence and the production of nuclear weapons.[69] They have fought for stricter anti-pollution legislation and campaigned for animal rights.[70] It is hard to find a pantheist who is not vocal about his or her moral beliefs. Pantheists must explain where intelligence and morality come from. Could intelligence and morality have been caused by a non-intelligent and non-moral being? It appears more probable that the Ultimate Cause of intelligence and morality must Himself be an intelligent and moral Being.[71]

Fourth, why should anyone accept the pantheistic claim that the world is an illusion? Does not common sense and experience favor the reality of the physical world? Why should anyone embrace pantheism without any evidence when common sense and experience teach otherwise?[72]

For these four reasons it appears that pantheism as a world view has failed. If an alternative to theism is to be found, one must look elsewhere.

Panentheism: A God who is both Finite and Infinite

Panentheism has been described as the belief that the universe is God's body.[73] In this world view, God is conceived of as having two poles to His existence. In His potential pole, He is infinite, unchanging, and eternal. In His actual pole, He is finite, changing, and temporal.[74] Unlike pantheism, panentheism views God as personal.[75]

---

[69]Walter Martin, *The New Age Cult* (Minneapolis: Bethany House Publishers, 1989), 65.

[70]Ibid.

[71]Geisler, *Apologetics*, 247-248.

[72]Geisler and Watkins, 102.

[73]Ibid., 108.

[74]Ibid.

However, panentheism fails for several reasons. First, God cannot be both infinite and finite. This would be the same as saying that God is both unlimited and limited,[76] and this is an obvious contradiction. The Christian concept of God is one of an infinite God in His basic nature.[77] Panentheism, on the other hand, holds the contradictory concept of a God who is both infinite and finite in His basic nature.

Second, panentheism is again contradictory when it declares God to be both eternal (without a beginning) and temporal (with a beginning).[78] One cannot have it both ways. Either God is eternal or God is temporal. In the Christian doctrine of the incarnation, the eternal God added a temporal nature to his eternal nature.[79] This involves no contradiction, but, in the case of panentheism, a contradiction is evident. If the eternal pole of God caused the temporal pole of God to come into existence, then it would make more sense for the panentheist to refer to the temporal pole not as God, but as God's creation. But then the panentheist would cease to be a panentheist. In fact, he would then be a theist.[80]

Third, panentheism teaches that God actualizes His own potentialities. However, this is impossible. No potentiality can actualize itself. For instance, empty cups cannot fill themselves. For a potentiality to become actual, something actual must actualize it. As a result, the panentheistic god, if it existed, would need the theistic God to actualize its potential to exist.[81] Therefore, panentheism also fails as a world view.

---

[75]Ibid., 136.

[76]Ibid.

[77]Millard J. Erickson, *Christian Theology* (Grand Rapids: Baker Book House, 1985), 272.

[78]Geisler and Watkins, 139.

[79]Erickson, 735.

[80]Geisler and Watkins, 21.

[81]Geisler, *Apologetics*, 208-209.

Deism: A God without Miracles

Deism is the world view that promotes the belief in a God who created the universe but no longer has any dealings with it.[82] The deist believes that God allows the world to operate on its own in accordance with natural laws that He has set in motion.[83] God does not perform miracles or interrupt the natural course of events.[84]

Thomas Jefferson, Benjamin Franklin, and Thomas Paine were deists of the eighteenth century.[85] Though deism is not as popular as it once was, similar views are held today by many Unitarians and religious humanists.[86]

Several objections to deism deserve mention. First, deists deny a miracle-working God. Yet, they admit one of God's greatest supernatural works when they affirm His work of creation. If God could create the entire universe out of nothing, then could He not perform lesser miracles?[87]

Second, if God cared enough to create the universe, then why doesn't He care enough to be involved with it?[88] And, third, the deistic view of natural laws is outdated. Natural laws are now considered by scientists to be descriptive of the general way nature acts. No longer are natural laws thought to prescribe what can and cannot happen in

---

[82]Ibid., 147-148.

[83]Ibid.

[84]Ibid.

[85]Ibid., 148.

[86]Ibid., 181.

[87]Ibid.

[88]Ibid., 182.

nature.[89] Natural laws cannot automatically rule out miracles, just as the occurrence of usual events does not disprove the possibility of unusual events occurring.[90]

In the seventeenth and eighteenth centuries, deism was a strong movement.[91] Much of its popularity was due to the belief that the science of that day had proven miracles to be impossible.[92] However, now that this misconception has been overturned, deism is no longer the attractive world view that it once was.

Finite Theism

Finite Godism is a world view that accepts the existence of a god. However, it believes He is limited.[93] Adherents differ as to how God is limited. Some believe He is limited in His power.[94] Others consider Him limited in His knowledge or His goodness.[95]

Devotees of Finite Godism usually promote their world view as the answer to the problem of evil.[96] They reason that an all-good and all-powerful God would not allow evil and innocent humans to suffer in the world.[97] Rabbi Harold Kushner, author of *When Bad Things Happen to Good People*, holds this view. He believes that evil proves God is not

---

[89]Ibid., 181.

[90]Ibid.

[91]Ibid., 148.

[92]Ibid., 181.

[93]Ibid., 188.

[94]Ibid.

[95]Ibid., 189-190.

[96]Ibid., 188.

[97]Ibid.

perfect and that He is limited in power.[98] For if God could prevent it, reasons Kushner, God would not allow the innocent to suffer.[99] Kushner asks others to forgive God for His failures.[100]

Several responses have been given to overthrow belief in the existence of a finite God. First, all finite existence needs a cause for its continuing existence.[101] Finite beings are, by definition, limited beings. And limited beings, precisely because of their limitations, must depend on other beings to keep them in existence. In fact, if everything that exists is limited and dependent, then nothing would now exist. For there must exist an infinite Being that is the cause of the continuing existence of all finite and dependent beings. In other words, a finite God would depend on an infinite God for its existence. However, a finite God would not be God after all. Only the infinite Being is God.[102]

Second, a finite God doesn't deserve worship.[103] Only a being that is ultimately worthy is deserving of worship. A God with limitations is surely not ultimately worthy. Only an infinite Being is deserving of worship.

Third, evil does not prove that God must be limited.[104] An all-good and all-powerful God may choose to allow evil and human suffering for the purpose of a greater good. What exactly this greater good may entail in specific cases may remain a mystery to finite beings, but, the wisdom of an infinite Being far transcends the wisdom of finite beings (Isaiah

---

[98]Harold S. Kushner, *When Bad Things Happen to Good People* (New York: Avon Books, 1981), 148.

[99]Ibid., 134.

[100]Ibid., 147-148.

[101]Geisler and Watkins, 211-212.

[102]Ibid., 212.

[103]Ibid.

[104]Ibid., 212-213.

55:8-9). A child may question the decision of his parents to allow him to receive surgery. But he does not have access to the amount of information that his parents have, and he does not see that the present pain he is enduring is for the purpose of future healing. The relationship of mankind to God is analogous to the relationship of this child to his parents. Also, God may defeat evil in the future (as the Bible teaches). In fact, only an infinite God can guarantee the ultimate defeat of evil. A finite God cannot.[105]

In short, finite godism leaves one with a god who is no God at all. For he, like the rest of the universe, needs a cause. He is not worthy of worship, and he cannot guarantee the defeat of evil. A god who needs help and forgiveness deserves only sympathy, not worship.

Polytheism

Polytheism is the world view that teaches the existence of more than one god.[106] Many Eastern religions accept the existence of many gods. This includes certain forms of Hinduism, Confucianism, Shintoism, Taoism, and Jainism.[107] Western thought is itself not without polytheistic belief systems. Ancient Greek mythology expressed polytheistic themes.[108] Several cult groups such as Mormonism, Scientology, and the Unification Church spread polytheism in the West today.[109]

Polytheism fails for the following reasons. Either all the gods are finite or at least one of them is infinite. They cannot all be finite. If they

---

[105]Ibid., 212.

[106]Ibid., 217.

[107]Ibid., 218.

[108]Ibid.

[109]Ibid.

are all finite beings, then they would need an infinite Being to ground their existence, but, then this infinite Being would be God.[110]

So there must exist at least one infinite Being. It is not possible that there exist more than one infinite Being. If more than one infinite Being existed, they would limit one another's existence. One infinite Being could prevent the other infinite Being(s) from accomplishing its goals. But then these beings would not be infinite since they would be limited by another's power. Therefore, there must exist one, and only one, infinite Being.[111] This one infinite Being would alone be God. Therefore, Polytheism fails in its attempt to explain reality.

Skepticism not a Viable Option

All world views, except for theism, have been shown to be failures. They are self-contradictory and fail to explain the available evidence. If theism, the only remaining world view, also fails, then skepticism would be the only possible alternative. However, skepticism also fails.

If one decides to be a skeptic, then he has chosen to suspend judgment on all things. He has failed to suspend judgment on his choice to be a skeptic.[112] This, of course, is contradictory. Also, no one can consistently live like a skeptic. For example, if someone suspended judgment on what he should eat, then he would eventually starve to death.[113]

Skepticism and all non-theistic world views have been shown to fail. A positive defense of theism (i.e., the belief in one, personal Creator God who is able to perform miracles) will be discussed below.

---

[110]Norman Geisler, *Thomas Aquinas* (Grand Rapids: Baker Book House, 1991), 130.

[111]Ibid.

[112]Geisler and Feinberg, 93-94.

[113]Ibid., 94.

Chapter Three:
The Case for God

The God of theism is the eternal uncaused Cause of all else that exists. This Being is personal (i.e., a moral and intelligent being) and unlimited in all His attributes. This Being is separate from His creation (transcendent), but He is also involved with it (immanent).

This booklet will not attempt to prove God's existence beyond all reasonable doubt. Instead, it will merely be argued that theism (belief in God) is more reasonable than atheism (the denial of God's existence) when we look at several common aspects of human experience. The preponderance of the evidence favors theism, not atheism. Theism is a more adequate explanation of human experience than the attempted atheistic explanation. Though it can be shown, as Thomas Aquinas has done, that infinite Being (i.e., God) *must* exist in order to ground the continuing existence of all finite beings, this booklet will merely provide strong evidence that theism is far more plausible than atheism.

The Beginning of the Universe

This argument is called the kalam cosmological argument for God's existence. Saint Bonaventure utilized this argument.[114] William Lane Craig and J. P. Moreland are two modern proponents of it.[115] This argument is as follows: 1) whatever began to exist must have a cause, 2) the universe began to exist, 3) therefore, the universe had a cause.[116]

Premise #1 uses the law of causality—non-being cannot cause being. In other words, from nothing, nothing comes. Since nothing is nothing, it can do nothing. Therefore, it can cause nothing. Hence, whatever began to exist needs a cause for its existence.[117]

Premise #2 contends that the universe had a beginning. Scientific evidence for the beginning of the universe includes the second law of thermodynamics (energy deterioration) and the Big Bang Model. The second law of thermodynamics is one of the most firmly established laws of modern science. It states that the amount of usable energy in a closed system is running down. This means that someday in the finite future all the energy in the universe will be useless (unless there is intervention from "outside" the universe). In other words, if left to itself, the universe will have an end. But if the universe is going to have an end, it had to have a beginning.[118] At one time, in the finite past, all the energy in the universe was usable. Since the universe is winding down, it must have been wound up. The universe is not eternal; it had a

---

[114]Frederick Copleston, *A History of Philosophy*, vol. 2 (New York: Image Books, 1993), 262-265.

[115]William Lane Craig, *Reasonable Faith* (Wheaton: Crossway Books, 1994), 91-122. J. P. Moreland, Scaling the Secular City (Grand Rapids: Baker Book House, 1987), 22-42.

[116]Craig, *Reasonable Faith*, 92.

[117]Ibid., 92-94.

[118]Ibid., 113-116.

beginning. Since it had a beginning, it needs a cause, for from nothing, nothing comes.

It should also be noted that, due to energy deterioration, if the universe is eternal it would have reached a state of equilibrium in which no change is possible an infinite amount of time ago. All of the universe's energy would already have been used up. Obviously, this is not the case. Therefore, the universe had a beginning.[119]

The Big Bang Model also indicates that the universe had a beginning.[120] In 1929, astronomer Edwin Hubble discovered that the universe is expanding at the same rate in all directions. As time moves forward the universe is growing apart. But this means that if we go back in time the physical universe would get smaller and smaller. Eventually, if we go back far enough in the past, the entire universe would be what scientists call "a point of infinite density" or "a point of dimensionless space." However, if something physical is infinitely dense, it is non-existent, for physical, existent things can only be finitely small. The same can be said for points of dimensionless space. If a physical point has no dimensions, it is non-existent for it takes up no space. Therefore, if the Big Bang Model is correct, it shows that the universe began out of nothing a finite time ago.

There have been two main attempts to refute the beginning of the universe. The first is called the steady-state model.[121] This view holds that the universe never had a beginning. Instead, it always existed in the same state. Because of the mounting evidence for the Big Bang Model, this view has been abandoned my most of its adherents.

The second attempt to evade the beginning of the universe is called the oscillating model.[122] This model teaches that, at some point

---

[119]Ibid.

[120]Ibid., 100-113.

[121]Ibid., 102-103.

[122]Ibid., 103-107.

during the universe's expansion, gravity will halt the expansion and pull everything back together again. From that point there will be another big bang. This process will be repeated over and over again throughout all eternity. However, the oscillating model fails. First, there is no known principle of physics that would reverse the collapse of the universe and cause another big bang. Second, current scientific research has shown that the universe is not dense enough for gravity to pull it back together again. And third, even if it could be proven that several big bangs have occurred, the second law of thermodynamics would still require that there was a first big bang.[123]

Many scientists accept the beginning of the universe, but believe that it does not need a cause. The evidence proposed by these scientists consists of speculation dealing with quantum physics (the study of subatomic particles). Appeal is made to Heisenberg's Principle of Indeterminacy in order to claim that quantum particles pop into existence out of nothing, entirely without a cause. However, Heisenberg's Principle does not necessitate such an absurd interpretation.[124] Simply because scientists cannot presently find the causes does not mean that the causes do not exist. All that Heisenberg's Principle states is that scientists are presently unable to accurately predict where a specific subatomic particle will be at a given time. If this principle proved that events can occur without causes then this would destroy one of the pillars of modern science—the principle of causality (every event must have an adequate cause). It seems obvious to me that the principle of causality is on firmer epistemological ground than the belief that things can pop into existence without a cause.

Non-being cannot cause being. If the universe had a beginning, then it needs a cause. Besides this scientific evidence there is also philosophical evidence for the beginning of the universe. If the universe is eternal, then there would be an actual infinite number of events in

---

[123]Ibid.

[124]William Lane Craig and Quentin Smith, *Theism, Atheism, and Big Bang Cosmology* (Oxford: Oxford University Press, 1993), 142-146.

time. However, as Zeno's paradoxes have shown, it is impossible to traverse an actual infinite set of points.[125] If we assume the existence of an infinite amount of actual points between two locations, then we can never get from location A to location B, since no matter how many points we have traversed, there will still be an infinite number of points left. If the universe is eternal, then there must exist an actual infinite set of events in the past, but then it would be impossible to reach the present moment. Since the present moment has been reached, there cannot be an actual infinite set of events in the past. There could only be a finite number. Therefore, there had to be a first event. Hence, the universe had a beginning.

It should also be noted that if it is possible for an actual infinite set to exist outside of a mind, contradictions and absurdities would be generated. To illustrate this point, let us look at two infinite sets. Set A consists of all numbers, both odd and even. Set B contains only all the odd numbers. Set A and Set B are equal since they both have an infinite number of members. Still, Set A has twice the number of members as Set B since Set A contains both odd and even numbers, while Set B contains only odd numbers. It is a clear contradiction to say that Set A and Set B have an equal amount of members, while Set A has twice as many members as Set B. Therefore, actual infinite sets cannot exist outside the mind. Actual sets existing outside the mind can only be potentially infinite, not actually infinite. These sets can be added to indefinitely; still, we will never reach an actual infinite by successive addition.[126] Therefore, the universe cannot have an infinite number of events in the past. The universe had a beginning.

Since the universe had to have a beginning, it had to have a cause. For from nothing, nothing comes. But if the universe needs a cause, what if the cause of the universe also needs a cause? Could we not have an infinite chain of causes and effects stretching backwards in time throughout all eternity? Obviously, the answer is no, for we have already

---

[125]Craig, *Reasonable Faith*, 94-100.
[126]Ibid., 98-100.

shown that an actual infinite set existing outside of a mind is impossible. Therefore, an infinite chain of causes and effects is also impossible. There had to be a first uncaused Cause of the universe. This uncaused Cause would be eternal, without beginning or end. Only eternal and uncaused existence can ground the existence of the universe.[127]

In short, there are only four possible explanations as to why the universe exists. First, the universe could be an eternal chain of causes and effects. Second, the universe could have popped into existence out of nothing without a cause. Third, the universe could merely be an illusion. And, fourth, the universe could have been caused to come into existence by an eternal, uncaused Cause (i.e., God). Strong evidence has been provided against the first and second options, as well as strong argumentation in favor of the fourth option. The third option is not a viable position, since it cannot be affirmed without contradiction. Those who claim the universe is an illusion usually contend that all of reality is one mind. However, the communicating of this view necessitates and assumes the existence of two or more minds. Hence, the statement that the universe is an illusion is self-refuting. Therefore, the most plausible explanation for the existence of the universe is that is has an uncaused Cause.

Today, most knowledgeable atheists acknowledge that the universe had a beginning. Still, they argue that the universe did not have a cause—it popped into existence, out of nothing, totally without a cause. "In the beginning God created the universe" seems much more plausible then "In the beginning nothing created the universe." Atheists used to argue, before Hubble showed the universe is expanding, that the universe is eternal, it had no beginning, and hence it doesn't need a cause. Now, atheists admit the universe had a beginning, but still argue that it doesn't need a cause. However, this seems highly improbable. In fact, it is impossible, for no possibility can exist without something actual existing. It makes sense to say that if something actual exists (i.e., God), then He could have had the potential to create. But, if absolutely nothing exists, it (i.e., nothing) had no potential or power to create. Only

---

[127]Ibid., 116-117.

actual things have potential or power; nothing lacks the potential to create, or do anything else for that matter. Since the universe had a beginning, theism (belief in God) is far more reasonable than atheism.

Therefore, since the universe had a beginning, it must have had an uncaused Cause. Several attributes of the uncaused Cause of the universe can be discovered through examination of the universe. Intelligent life exists in the universe. Since intelligence is a perfection found in the universe, the ultimate Cause of the universe must also be an intelligent Being, for intelligence cannot come from non-intelligence. No one has ever presented a reasonable explanation as to how intelligence could evolve from mindless nature.[128]

Morality also exists in the universe, for without morality, there would be no such thing as right and wrong. However, the moral judgments we make show that we do believe there are such things as right and wrong. Still, nature is non-moral.[129] No one holds a rock morally responsible for tripping him. There is no way that mere "molecules in motion" could produce moral values. Since nature is non-moral but morality exists in the universe, the Cause of the universe must be a moral Being.[130]

The moral law is not invented by individuals, for one individual condemns the actions of another. If morality is relative and subjective, then no one could call the actions of Adolph Hitler wrong.[131] Nor could society be the cause of moral laws, since societies often pass judgment on one another (America and the Allies denounced the actions of Nazi Germany).[132] Even world consensus fails to qualify for the source of

---

[128]Francis A. Schaeffer, *Trilogy* (Wheaton: Crossway Books, 1990), 283.

[129]C. S. Lewis, *Mere Christianity* (New York: Collier Books, 1952), 19, 26-29.

[130]Geisler and Corduan, 112.

[131]Ibid., 113.

[132]Ibid.

moral values since the world consensus once held slavery to be morally defensible. Only an absolute moral Lawgiver who is qualitatively above man can be the Cause of a moral law that stands above man and judges his actions. This moral Lawgiver must be eternal and unchanging since we make moral judgments about the past (slavery, evil treatment of women). Therefore, the uncaused Cause of the universe must be an intelligent, moral Being. This means that God must be a personal Being.[133]

Atheists like Richard Dawkins refuse to accept any supernatural Cause for the universe. Hence, they are willing to believe in "chance" as the cause of the universe.[134] However, there is a problem with this kind of reasoning. For, if absolutely nothing existed before the beginning of the universe, then chance did not exist as well. For there are no possibilities (i.e., chances) if there is nothing actual. If a person is willing to go where the evidence leads, then he will conclude that belief in God as the cause of the universe is more plausible than belief in "chance."

The belief that God created the universe is far more believable than the belief that the universe came into existence, out of nothing, totally without a cause. It is either "In the beginning God created the heavens and the earth," or "In the beginning nothing created the heavens and the earth." The former is far more plausible than the latter. Concerning the origin of the universe, theism (belief in God) is more reasonable than atheism (the denial of God's existence).

The Continuing Existence of the Universe

This argument for God's existence derives its substance from Thomas Aquinas' five ways to prove God's existence.[135] Experience

---

[133]Geisler, *Christian Apologetics*, 249.

[134]Richard Dawkins, *The God Delusion* (Boston: Houghton Mifflin Company, 2006), 145-147, 158.

[135]Thomas Aquinas, *Summa Theologiae*, 1a. 2.3.

shows us that limited, dependent (contingent) beings exist. These limited, dependent beings need other beings for their continued existence. For example, I depend on air, water, and food to sustain my existence. However, adding limited, dependent beings will never give us an independent and unlimited whole. Therefore, the sum total of limited, dependent beings is itself limited and dependent. (If each individual part of a floor is wood, then the whole floor will be wood. Likewise, if each part of the universe is dependent, then the entire universe is dependent.) Hence, the ultimate Cause of the continuing existence of all limited, dependent beings must be unlimited and independent (i.e., a Necessary Being).

Here is another way of stating this argument. If everything that exists has the possibility of not existing, then, given enough time, nothing will exist. For, given enough time, every possibility will be actualized. But, this also means that if we were to go backwards in time, eventually we would reach a point in which the same situation would have obtained. Again, nothing would exist. But, since from nothing, nothing comes, something must have always existed with no possibility of non-existence in order to ground the continued existence of all beings that have the possibility of non-existence.[136] The Christian believes God to be this Necessary Being, a being with no possibility of non-existence. This Necessary Being is by definition unlimited and totally independent.

There cannot be two or more unlimited and independent beings since, if there were, they would limit one another's existence, but then they would not be unlimited. Therefore, there can only be one unlimited and independent Being. Also, for two beings to differ, one of the beings would have to have something the other being lacks, or lack something the other being has. This also shows that there cannot be two or more unlimited beings. For a Being to be unlimited, it has to have every possible perfection and must have each of these perfections to an unlimited degree. But, for another being to differ from this unlimited Being, it would have to lack at least one of the perfections or have at

---

[136]Ibid.

least one of the perfections to a less than unlimited degree. But, then this being that differs from the unlimited Being would not itself be unlimited. Again, only one unlimited Being can exist—there cannot be two or more unlimited Beings.[137]

This unlimited Being must have all its attributes in an unlimited way. Otherwise, it would not be an unlimited Being. This Being must be all-powerful, for He is the source of all the power in the universe. No other power can limit Him. He is eternal for He is not limited by time. He is everywhere present since He is not limited by space. He is immaterial since He is not limited by matter. This Being must be all-good since He is not limited by evil. He must also be all-knowing since He is not limited by ignorance.[138]

Since mindless nature works towards goals (such as acorns always becoming oak trees and not something else), there must be an intelligent Designer overseeing natural processes.[139] Without intelligent design, nature's processes would be left to chance. There would be no orderly patterns that could be described as natural laws. Therefore, this infinite and independent Being, whom all finite and dependent beings depend upon for their continued existence, must be an intelligent Being.

Not only does Dawkins invoke "chance" to explain the beginning of the universe, but he also appeals to "chance" to explain the continuing existence of the universe. It is more reasonable to believe that God causes the continuing existence of all the limited beings that exist, than it is to believe that limited beings continue to exist by random chance.

The Design and Order Found in the Universe

The order, design, and complexity found in the universe strongly imply that the universe is not a random, chaotic throwing together of

---

[137]Geisler, *Christian Apologetics*, 250.

[138]Ibid., 247-249.

[139]Thomas Aquinas, 1a. 2.3.

34

atoms; rather, it is the product of intelligent design. And, as the product of intelligent design, it necessitates the existence of an intelligent Designer.

Contemporary scientists have found numerous evidences for design in the universe.[140] A few examples will suffice. First, the slightest variation in the expansion rate of the universe would render the universe incapable of sustaining life. Second, British scientists Hoyle and Wickramasinghe estimated that the chances of life evolving from the random shuffling of organic molecules is virtually zero. They calculated that there is only one chance in ten to the twentieth power to form a single enzyme, and just one chance in ten to the forty-thousandth power to produce the approximately 2,000 enzymes that exist. However, Hoyle and Wickramasinghe point out that the production of enzymes is only one step in the generation of life. Therefore, they concluded there must be some type of Cosmic Intelligence to explain the origin of life.[141] Hoyle compared the probability of life spontaneously generating from non-life as equivalent to the chances of a tornado producing a Boeing 747 from a junkyard.[142]

The cell is the basic unit of life. The DNA molecule of a single-celled animal contains enough complex information to fill one-thousand complete sets of encyclopedia.[143] An explosion in a print shop will never produce one volume of an encyclopedia. That amount of information necessitates an intelligent cause. Also, the human brain contains more genetic information than the world's largest libraries.[144] There is no way

---

[140]J. P. Moreland and Kai Nielsen, *Does God Exist? The Great Debate* (Nashville: Thomas Nelson Publishers, 1990), 35-36.

[141]Ibid., 143.

[142]Ibid., 35.

[143]Norman L. Geisler and J. Kerby Anderson, *Origin Science* (Grand Rapids: Baker Book House, 1987), 162.

[144]Ibid.

that this amount of information could be produced by mere chance. Intelligent intervention is needed.

Third, astrophysicist Hugh Ross listed twenty-five narrowly defined parameters that the universe had to have in order for life to be possible.[145] Ross also pointed out thirty-two narrowly defined parameters for life concerning the earth, its moon, its sun, and its galaxy.[146] For instance, if the distance between the earth and the sun was to differ by just two percent in either direction, no life on earth would be possible.[147] These parameters for life on earth clearly show evidence of design and purpose. Scientists refer to this as the "anthropic principle" (from the Greek word "anthropos" for man) because the universe seems to have been fine-tuned for the purpose of supporting human life on the planet earth.

The theistic hypothesis of intelligent design is obviously more plausible than the atheistic hypothesis of random chance. Even atheist Richard Dawkins admits that the universe has the appearance of being designed. But, then he calls design an "illusion" and speculates about multiple, non-observable universes. Again, he invokes chance.[148]

However, if the universe appears as if it was designed, then it is more plausible to believe that it was designed and not the product of blind chance. Science begins with the world of appearances, not wild speculation about non-observable universes. Dawkins' multiverse theory is closer to science fiction than to good science. Whenever there is evidence for a supernatural cause, he invokes all-powerful chance to save the day. This is not evidence against God; rather, it is evidence of Dawkins' flight from God and refusal to accept any evidence for God.

---

[145]Hugh Ross, *The Creator and the Cosmos* (Colorado Springs: NavPress, 1993), 111-114.

[146]Ibid., 129-132.

[147]Ibid., 127.

[148]Dawkins, 157-158.

It is an explaining away of the scientific evidence—it is not an acceptance of the scientific evidence.

The Possibility of Human Knowledge

The theist claims to know something (i.e., that God exists), and the atheist claims to know something (i.e., that God does not exist). Even the agnostic claims to know something (i.e., that the supposed evidence for God's existence is insufficient). However, it seems that only theism (the belief in a personal God) justifies the possibility of human knowledge. C. S. Lewis pointed out that if our reason (i.e., our thinking ability) came from non-rational causes, then there is no justification for trusting in our reason. However, theism entails the doctrine that a rational God created man in His image (i.e., a rational being) and a coherent universe so that through reason man could find out about the universe in which he lives. Remove the rational God of theism from the equation, and the basis for human knowledge appears to crumble. It is hard to imagine how human knowledge and reasoning ability could have evolved into existence from non-rational matter. Again, theism is more rational than atheism.[149]

The Reality of Universal, Unchanging Truths

The denial of absolute truth is self-refuting, for if the statement "there is no absolute truth" is true, then it would be an absolute truth. Complete agnosticism is also self-refuting, for to say that man cannot know truth is a claim to know this "truth." Therefore, there is absolute truth and it is possible for man to know truth.

Some truths are universal, unchanging, and eternal. An example of this would be the mathematical truth "1 + 1 = 2." We do not invent mathematical truths—we discover them. This also applies to the laws of logic (i.e., the law of non-contradiction, the law of excluded middle, the law of identity, etc.). These truths stand above human minds and judge

---

[149]C. S. Lewis, *Miracles* (New York: Collier Books, 1960), 14-22, 55-62.

human minds. For instance, if we add 1 + 1 and we conclude with 3, the eternal truth that 1 + 1 = 2 will declare us wrong. However, Augustine argued that it is not likely that human, fallible minds are the ultimate cause of universal, unchanging, eternal truths. Augustine concluded that an unchanging, eternal Mind must be the ultimate source of these truths.[150]

Atheism has no basis for eternal, unchanging truths. If atheism is "true," then there may have been a time when 1 + 1 equaled 3. There may also have been a time when torturing innocent babies was good. In fact, if atheism is true, there may have been a time when the statement "God exists" was true.

Atheism implies that there is no truth. Hence, if atheism is true, then it cannot be true, for there is no such thing as truth. Therefore, the existence of truth is more plausible in a theistic universe than in a world without God. The new atheists pride themselves in knowing the truth. Yet, their world view has no place for truth. Truth is rather strange furniture for a universe without God. Consistent atheists are materialists; they believe that only material, physical things exist. Universal truths are not physical things. When the atheist believes in truth it is because he is borrowing capital from the Christian world view.

The Existence of Absolute Moral Laws

Everyone makes moral value judgments when they call the actions of another person wrong. When they do this, they appeal to a moral law. This moral law could not originate with each individual, for then one could not call the actions of another person, such as Adolph Hitler, wrong.

The moral law is not a creation of each society, for then one society cannot call the actions of another society, such as Nazi Germany, wrong. The moral law does not come from a world consensus, for world consensus is often mistaken. The world once thought that the earth was

---

[150]Augustine, *On Free Will*, 2.6.

flat, the sun revolved around the earth, and slavery was morally acceptable. Appealing to society or world consensus will never create an adequate cause for the moral law and the moral judgments humans make. Appealing to society or world consensus only quantitatively adds men and women. What is needed is a moral law qualitatively above man. This moral law must be eternal and unchanging so that one can condemn the actions of the past (i.e., slavery, the holocaust, etc.).

The moral law qualitatively above man is not descriptive of the way things are (as is the case with natural laws). The moral law must be prescriptive—it describes the way things ought to be.[151] Prescriptive laws need a Prescriber. Therefore, a moral Lawgiver must exist, and this Lawgiver must be eternal and unchanging.

Humans are accountable to this moral Lawgiver that stands above all mankind. Atheist Sigmund Freud failed miserably in his attempt to explain the universal experience of guilt.[152] The best explanation for the guilt all humans experience is the fact that we know we stand guilty before a righteous and holy God. Therefore, when we make moral value judgments, whether it involves self-judgment (a guilty conscience) or judgment of another person, we appeal to a transcendent objective moral law. This is a strong indication that there exists a transcendent moral Lawgiver.

Therefore, theism is a more plausible explanation for our moral experience than atheism is. In fact, atheists are very inconsistent when they pronounce moral value judgments against Christianity, since they have no real basis within their atheism for morality.

---

[151]C. S. Lewis, *Mere Christianity*, 27-28.

[152]Ninian Smart, *The Religious Experience of Mankind* (New York: Charles Scribner's Sons, 1976), 40-41.

The Absurdity of Life Without God

Each of us thirsts for something more; life on earth never fully satisfies. Only the God of the Bible can fully satisfy man's deepest needs. What hope can an atheist offer mankind? People on their deathbeds don't usually call an atheist to comfort them-normally a preacher or a priest is summoned. Even if an atheist could guarantee us seventy years of happiness, what good would that be when compared with the eternity of non-existence that follows? If there is no God who sits enthroned, then Hitler will not be punished for his evil deeds, and Mother Theresa will not be rewarded for her generous works of charity. If there is no God, then a million years from now what would it matter if you were a Hitler or a Mother Theresa? What difference would it make?[153]

Does life have any ultimate meaning if there is no God? If nonexistence is what awaits us, can we really make sense of life? You live and then you die. There are no eternal consequences. Hitler and Mother Theresa have the same destiny. We all finish our meaningless journeys in total nothingness. The famous atheist Bertrand Russell wrote:

That man is the product of causes which had no prevision of the end they were achieving; that his origin, his growth, his hopes and fears, his loves and his beliefs, are but the outcome of accidental collocations of atoms; that no fire, no heroism, no intensity of thought and feeling, can preserve an individual life beyond the grave; that all the labors of the ages, all the devotion, all the inspiration, all the noonday brightness of human genius, are destined to extinction in the vast death of the solar system, and that the whole temple of man's achievement must inevitably be buried beneath the debris of a universe in ruins . . .[154]

---

[153]Norman Geisler and Frank Turek, *I Don't Have Enough Faith to be an Atheist* (Wheaton: Crossway Books, 2004), 176-179.

[154]Bertrand Russell, *Why I Am Not a Christian* (New York: Simon and Schuster, 1957), 107.

Immediately following this statement, Russell referred to his atheistic philosophy as "the firm foundation of unyielding despair."[155] Without God, life is without meaning.

However, if there is a God, then there is hope. The God of the Bible guarantees the defeat of evil and the triumph of good. He guarantees that Hitler will receive his punishment and Mother Theresa will receive her reward. God gives life meaning, for how we choose to live our lives on earth brings eternal consequences. God is our reason to be optimistic about the future. Only He can overcome our fear of death; only He can defeat evil. Without God, meaningless existence is all we face. Without God, there is no hope.

Without belief in God and life after death, atheism fails to supply man with the necessary ingredients for meaningful existence. Yet, most people live like life has meaning. Again, theism is more reasonable than atheism. The new atheists live like life is meaningful; they act as if their hard work will have lasting effects. They act as if the books they write are worth the trouble. They do not act like they believe that someday the universe will die and everything they ever accomplished will die with it. Without realizing it, they act as if theism is true.

Respect for Human Life and Human Rights

If atheism is true, then man is mere molecules in motion. He has no greater value than the animals. In fact, human life would be no more sacred than the existence of a rock. Yet, we act as if human life has more value than the life of animals or the existence of rocks. If the material universe is all there is, then man is just a material part of the universe. There seems to be no basis from which to argue for human rights or the sanctity of human life. Even our founding fathers (who were not always consistent with their ideals) grounded their view of unalienable human rights in their belief that "all men are created equal." The most

---

[155]Ibid.

reasonable explanation for our common conception of human rights is the biblical teaching that human life has value since we were created in God's image.

Atheism offers no real foundation for human rights.[156] It must again borrow from the Christian world view to posit human rights. Or, the atheist might believe that human rights are man-made—they come from human governments. But, this is probably not a good move for the atheist to make. Research has shown that human government is the number one serial killer of all time, killing well over 100 million innocent people in the twentieth century alone.[157] This is more deaths than have occurred in all of mankind's wars throughout history. Grounding human rights in human government is not a good idea. Human governments did not invent human rights; human rights come from God. God instituted human governments to protect our God-given human rights. If the new atheists have their way, human governments will be able to arbitrarily invent or remove human rights—we will be at the mercy of an all-powerful state. This did not work in the Soviet Union or Red China; it will not work in America either.

The Existence of Evil (Its Cause and Ultimate Defeat)

Atheists often argue that the existence or amount of evil in the world disproves the existence of the God of the Bible. There are two difficulties with this view. These difficulties cause the argument against God's existence from evil to backfire into an argument for God's existence.[158]

---

[156]Geisler and Turek, 175-176.

[157]R. J. Rummel, *Death by Government* (New Brunswick, NJ: Transaction Publishers, 1997), 9.

[158]William Lane Craig, *No Easy Answers* (Chicago: Moody Press, 1990), 99-100.

The first difficulty is that the atheist has no explanation for evil within his world view. If the atheist accepts the existence of evil, he must define what it is. If he denies the existence of evil, then he has no basis upon which to call any action evil. Evil can be defined as the perversion or corruption of that which is good. However, for good to be objectively real its existence must be grounded in something ultimately good. In other words, if the atheist acknowledges the existence of evil, his argument dissolves into a moral argument for God's existence. If he denies the existence of evil, his world view is morally bankrupt. If the atheist chooses to accept the existence of evil, but not seek its ultimate cause, then atheism becomes a non-explanation of evil. Hypotheses that do not attempt to explain the data in question should be abandoned. It is not enough to say that evil is "just there."

The second difficulty with the atheistic argument from the problem of evil is the fact that, if evil exists, atheism offers absolutely no solution to the problem. After a life of suffering and pain, people die and cease to exist. Eventually, the entire universe will cease to exist. I believe that the Christian solution to the problem of evil (the death, resurrection, and return of Christ) is the only hope that evil will be defeated. In fact, if Christianity is true, then Christianity guarantees the ultimate defeat of evil. The injustices of this life will be rectified in the hereafter. If atheism is true, death and extinction is the fate of all.

Human Free Will and Responsibility

If atheism is true, then it makes sense that the material world is all that exists. Non-material entities are rather strange furniture for a universe void of God. The physical realm would be all that exists. This would mean that humans do not have immaterial souls. Our choices would not really be free choices; instead, our decisions would merely be chemical reactions occurring in our brains. But, if this is the case,

43

then our choices are biologically determined—we are not free to choose our actions.[159]

If atheistic materialism is true, then we could not hold people responsible for their actions.[160] Someone's brain makes them serve others; another person's brain makes them slaughter others. Neither person is responsible for their choices or actions. If atheists really believe their world view is correct, then they should fight to close our prisons and set the prisoners free. For if human free will is an illusion (and consistent atheism says it is), then criminals are not responsible for their actions and therefore should not be punished for their actions. But, most atheists want to see criminals behind bars—they live like Christianity is true; they live like man is free and he is responsible for the choices he makes. Again, the theistic explanation is more plausible than the attempted atheistic explanation.

Feelings of Guilt

We all experience guilt when we do wrong, even if we sin when no one else is looking. Guilt is our innate knowledge of good and evil informing us that we have done evil. Even atheists experience guilt. They try to explain it away rather than admit that guilt tells us we have sinned before a holy God. One of the most famous atheists of all time— Sigmund Freud—devoted much of his thought and writing in an attempt to provide a naturalistic explanation of guilt. His wild speculation suggested that the first tribe of human males murdered their father due to their desire to have sex with their mothers. After killing their father, they felt guilty. Freud never actually explains why they felt guilty—the question as to why humans experience guilt remains.[161] It seems more

---

[159]Lee Strobel, *The Case for a Creator* (Grand Rapids: Zondervan Publishing House, 2004), 255-257.
[160]Ibid.

[161]Ninian Smart, 40.

44

likely that we experience guilt because we really are guilty. We have sinned before a holy God, and we need His deliverance. Guilt is a very strange piece of furniture in the universe if no God exists. Theism offers a far more plausible explanation for guilt than does atheism.

Conclusion of the Case for God

In the famous debate on the existence of God between Bertrand Russell and Frederick Copleston, the atheist Bertrand Russell stated concerning the existence of the universe, "I should say that the universe is just there, and that's all."[162] Atheism fails as an explanation of significant aspects of human experience. Theism is a far more reasonable hypothesis. If the atheist could say that "the universe is just there," could he not say that moral laws, design and order, universal truths, the human experience of guilt, the sanctity of human life, the possibility of human knowledge, and meaning in life are "just there" as well. To avoid looking for an explanation is not the same thing as the search for an explanation. In this sense, the theistic explanation is superior to the atheistic explanation, for the latter reduces to a non-explanation.

However, the atheist may choose to deny the reality of moral laws, design and order, universal truths, the human experience of guilt, the sanctity of human life, the possibility of human knowledge, and meaning in life. If the atheist takes this strategy, he cannot live consistently with the view that these things are not real. Even the atheist lives as if some things are wrong and other things are right. He lives as if human life is sacred, and life has meaning.

Rational statements only make sense within some type of rational context. The atheist, by arguing against God's existence, has removed the rational context (the universe as an effect of the rational God) for

---

[162]John Hick, ed., *The Existence of God* (New York: The Macmillian Company, 1964), 175.

rational discourse. He reasons against God; but, if there is no God, there is no reason.

Is it reasonable to believe that the universe popped into existence out of absolute nothingness—entirely without a cause? Or, is it rational to conclude that the universe is eternal despite the strong scientific and philosophical evidences that indicate that the universe had a beginning? Is the atheist justified in holding to the idea that time plus chance plus natural laws worked upon "primordial soup" until it eventually birthed a French philosopher who declared, "I think, therefore I am"? If atheism is true, then, given enough time, that's what occurred! Atheistic evolution only appears plausible in slow motion. Creation scientist Duane Gish once stated that when we hear about a frog instantly becoming a prince, we call it a fairy tale. But if we are told that a frog became a prince gradually over a period of several million years, we call this science!

From molecules in motion will never come moral values or the laws of logic. From a mound of dirt, a single thought will never be produced—no matter how much time is given. Chance plus time plus natural laws will never produce self-awareness or guilt. If no God exists then man is mere molecules in motion; from whence come human rights? If an innocent child is merely a random collection of atoms, can we really say that it is wrong to crush him? If there is no life after death and all we face is everlasting extinction, can this life really have meaning? What counsel can an atheist offer a suffering friend on his deathbed? Can we climb above despair if all we face is extinction? When the universe dies, all will die with it. If atheism is true, then human experience is a cruel joke. And, if life is a cruel joke, then why even bother to go on living? If there is no lasting hope for the future, they why pretend there is hope?

The theistic explanation is far superior to the atheistic explanation. The belief in God is a more reasonable explanation than atheism is for the common aspects of human experience that we have discussed. There are good reasons for believing in God. In fact, it is more reasonable to believe in God than it is to deny His existence. In fact, finite beings (i.e.,

46

the created universe) could not exist without being grounded in existence by an infinite Being (i.e., God).[163]

---

[163]Geisler, *Christian Apologetics*, 238-243.

Chapter Four:
Does Evil Disprove God?

One of the greatest obstacles keeping people from believing in God is the problem of evil.[164] Hence, many atheists use the existence of evil and human suffering as supposed evidence that God does not exist. But, this should not startle those who believe in God. For the problem of evil is nothing new—great Christian thinkers (i.e., Augustine, Aquinas, etc.) of the past have thoroughly dealt with this objection to Christianity.

The problem of evil can take several different forms. First, the metaphysical problem of evil asks how evil can exist in a world created by an all-good God.[165] Is God the cause of evil, or, is evil itself uncreated and eternal? Maybe evil is not real. Maybe it is simply an illusion.[166] The metaphysical problem deals with the origin and reality of evil in God's universe.

---

[164]Ronald Nash, *Faith and Reason* (Grand Rapids: Zondervan Publishing House, 1988), 177.

[165]Geisler and Corduan, *Philosophy of Religion* (Grand Rapids: Baker Book House, 1988), 318.

[166]Ibid.

Second, the moral problem of evil deals with the evil choices of personal beings.[167] This form of the problem argues that since an all-good God would want to destroy evil, and an all-powerful God is able to destroy evil, the existence of evil proves that no all-good, all-powerful God exists.[168] The Christian apologist defends the existence of an all-good and all-powerful God. Therefore, he will respond to this argument.

The third form of the problem of evil is called the physical problem of evil.[169] The physical problem of evil deals with incidents of natural disasters and innocent humans suffering.[170] How could God allow evil to occur that is not directly caused by the abuse of human free will?[171]

The fourth and final form of the problem of evil is not really a philosophical issue. It is the personal problem of evil.[172] The personal problem of evil is not a theoretical question about the existence of evil. Instead, it is a personal struggle with a traumatic experience in one's own life.[173] Examples of this would be the sudden and unexpected death of a loved one, a bitter divorce, the loss of a job, or the like. In these situations, the troubled person does not need philosophical answers. What is needed is encouragement, comfort, and biblical counsel.[174] Since this form of the problem of evil does not deal with philosophical discussion, it will not be dealt with in this booklet. The remainder of this booklet will deal with the first three forms of the problem of evil.

---

[167]Ibid., 333.

[168]Ibid.

[169]Ibid., 364.

[170]Ibid.

[171] Ibid.

[172]Nash, 179-180.

[173]Ibid.

[174]Ibid., 180.

The Metaphysical Problem of Evil

The metaphysical problem of evil can be stated as follows: 1) God created everything that exists, 2) evil exists, 3) therefore, God created evil.[175] There are several ways people respond to this argument. First, like the Christian Science Cult, some choose to deny the reality of evil.[176] They view evil as an illusion, but this entails a rejection of Christian Theism which clearly accepts the real existence of evil and offers Christ as its solution.[177] Therefore, viewing evil as an illusion is not an option for the Christian apologist.

A second possible response to the metaphysical problem is dualism. This is the view that God and evil are coeternal.[178] In this view, God did not create evil since evil is eternal. This view fails in that it makes evil a second ultimate being along with God. God would then no longer be infinite since He and evil would limit each other. However, the cosmological argument has shown that there must be an infinite Being to explain and ground all finite existence. There cannot be two infinite beings, for they would limit each other. If God and evil are both finite, then there would have to be an infinite cause for the existence of both. Dualism would only push the problem of evil further back. It does not offer any ultimate solution to the dilemma. Also, the acceptance of dualism entails a rejection of the existence of the God of the Bible. Therefore, it is not an option for the Christian theist.[179]

---

[175]Geisler and Corduan, 318.

[176]Mary Baker Eddy, *Science and Health with Key to the Scriptures* (Boston: The First Church of Christ, Scientist, 1971), 293, 447, 472, 480, 482.

[177]Geisler and Corduan, 318-319.

[178]Ibid., 319.

[179] Ibid., 319-320.

The Christian apologist must defend the reality of evil without proposing evil as eternal or as a creation of God.[180] Centuries ago, Saint Augustine dealt with this same problem. His proposed solution to the metaphysical problem of evil was that all things created by God are good. Nothing in its created nature is evil. Evil, therefore, cannot exist solely on its own. However, evil is real; it does exist. Still, it must exist in something good. Evil is a privation, a lack or absence of a good that should be there. Evil is a corruption or perversion of God's good creation. Blindness in a man is evil, for God created man to see. But, blindness in a rock is not evil, for God never meant rocks to have sight. Evil, according to Augustine, is a lack of a good that should be there. Augustine stated, "evil has no positive nature; what we call evil is merely the lack of something that is good."[181]

Augustine stated that God did not create evil; He merely created the possibility for evil by giving men and angels free will. When men and angels exercised their free will by disobeying God, they actualized the possibility for evil.[182]

Thomas Aquinas argued against the metaphysical problem of evil along the same lines as did Augustine.[183] This basic response has been the traditional Christian solution to the metaphysical problem of evil. God did not create evil, but, evil exists as a privation or corruption of that which is good. God cannot be blamed for evil. He is only responsible for creating the possibility of evil. When God gave angels and men free will, He created the possibility of evil. Fallen angels and fallen men are responsible for evil through their abuse of free will.[184]

---

[180]Ibid., 318-320.

[181]Augustine, *City of God*, 11.9, 12.3, 14.11, 22.1.

[182]Geisler and Corduan, 323-324.

[183]Thomas Aquinas, *Summa Theologiae: A Concise Translation*, edited by Timothy McDermott (Westminster, MD: Christian Classics, 1989), 91-92

[184]Geisler and Corduan, 320-330.

The Moral Problem of Evil

The moral problem of evil affirms that an all-good God would want to destroy evil, while an all-powerful God is able to destroy evil. Since evil exists, it is concluded that an all-good, all-powerful God does not exist.[185] Some people respond by denying God's existence (atheism). Others deny that God is all-powerful (finite theism). Rabbi Harold Kushner is an example of the latter. He argues that God is not all-powerful. Kushner declares that mankind needs to forgive God for His failures and help Him to combat evil.[186] Obviously, the options of atheism and finite theism are not viable for Christians. Christians must defend both God's omnipotence (all-powerfulness) and His infinite goodness. Therefore, the moral problem of evil must be answered in another way. Christian philosophers Geisler and Corduan offer several effective responses to the moral problem of evil.

First, there is an unnecessary time limit placed on God.[187] The argument against the existence of the theistic God from moral evil assumes that because evil exists God cannot be both all-good and all-powerful. However, what if an all-good and all-powerful God allowed evil for the purpose of a greater good? What if this God is also in the process of destroying evil and will someday complete the process?[188]

Second, God may have created the possibility of evil for the purpose of a greater good (human and angelic free will). God would not force His love on angels or mankind, for any attempt to force love on another is rape (and not really love at all).[189] Therefore, He gave men and angels

---

[185]Ibid., 333.

[186]Harold S. Kushner, *When Bad Things Happen to Good People* (New York: Avon Books, 1981), 129,134,145-148.

[187]Geisler and Corduan, 334.

[188]Ibid., 348.

[189]Ibid.

the freedom to accept or reject His love and His will. Free will necessitates the possibility of evil coming into the universe.[190] In fact, human and angelic free choices brought evil and human suffering into the world.

Third, God will use evil for good purposes. If evil did not exist, there could be no courage, for there would be nothing to fear. If evil did not exist, man could only love his friends; he could never learn to love even his enemies. Without evil, there would be no enemies.[191] Only an infinite God can know all the good He will bring out of evil (Isaiah 55:8-9).

Fourth, Geisler and Corduan argue that an all-good and all-powerful God is not required to create the best possible world. They reason that all He can be expected to do is create the best possible way to achieve the greatest possible world. Heaven is the greatest possible world.[192]

Several other points could also be made. First, the atheist usually denies the existence of objective evil since he knows that this would admit to the existence of the absolute moral law.[193] The atheist knows that once he acknowledges the absolute moral law, the existence of God (the absolute moral law Giver) surely will follow.[194] For evil to be objectively real, it must exist as a perversion of that which is ultimately good. To escape this conclusion, the atheist usually chooses to deny the existence of evil. Therefore, it is rather ironic that the atheist (who usually denies the existence of evil) attempts to use evil to disprove the existence of the God of the Bible. The presence of evil may be

---

[190]Ibid.

[191]Ibid.

[192]Ibid., 342-343.
[193]C. S. Lewis, *Mere Christianity* (New York: MacMillian Publishing Company, 1952), 34-39.

[194]Ibid.

problematic for all other world views (including Christian theism), but it is totally devastating to atheism. If there is no God, then there are also no objective moral values. The most consistent atheists, such as Nietzsche, have readily admitted this.[195]

Second, all world views must deal with the problem of evil, but the God of the Bible is the only guarantee that evil will ultimately be defeated.[196] The God of deism is no longer concerned with the problems of this world (such as evil).[197] In pantheism, evil is an illusion.[198] In atheism, there is no basis to call anything evil.[199] But, the biblical God guarantees that evil will be defeated through Christ's death, resurrection, and return (John 1:29; 1 Pet. 2:24; 3:18; Rom. 4:25; Isa. 9:6-7; 11:1-9; Zech. 9:9-10; Rev. 20:4-6).

Third, non-Christians act as if the existence of evil is an unexpected factor in the Christian world view, but this is not the case. God would not have given mankind the Bible had it not been for the problem of evil. If man had not fallen into sin in the garden, he would have had no need for salvation (Gen. 3:1-7; Rom. 3:10, 23; 5:12; 6:23). The Bible could actually be titled "God's Solution to the Problem of Evil."

In short, the solution to the moral problem of evil (how an all-good, all-powerful God can co-exist with evil) is that God gave humans and angels free will. It is the abuse of this free will by humans and angels that has brought evil and human suffering into existence. God created the possibility for evil (by giving man and angels free will), not evil itself.

---

[195]Friedrich Nietzsche, *The Portable Nietzsche*, ed. by Walter Kaufmann, (New York: Penguin Books, 1982), 228.

[196]Geisler and Watkins, *Worlds Apart* (Grand Rapids: Baker Book House, 1989), 41.

[197]Ibid., 148-149.

[198]Ibid., 99-100.

[199]Ibid., 59.

Christian philosopher Alvin Plantinga adds an important detail concerning the Christian response to the moral problem of evil. He writes that there are two ways Christians can respond to this dilemma. First, he may develop a free will theodicy. A theodicy is an attempt to explain what was God's reason (or reasons) for allowing evil. On the other hand, according to Plantinga, the Christian does not have to go that far. Instead of presenting a free will theodicy, he may develop a free will defense. In this case, rather than attempting to explain the reason as to why God allows evil and human suffering, the Christian can merely suggest a *possible* reason why God has allowed evil and human suffering.[200] The free will defense, according to Plantinga, is sufficient in itself to show that the existence of evil does not rule out the possible existence of the God of theism.[201]

In other words, since the problem of evil is an attempt to prove God's existence as being impossible, the Christian only needs to provide possible solutions to this problem. Once this is done, God's existence will have been shown to be possible. Further argumentation (as was discussed above) can then be presented to argue for God's existence with a higher degree of probability.[202]

The Physical Problem of Evil

The physical or natural problem of evil deals with evil not directly connected to the abuse of human freedom.[203] All physical or natural evil is at least indirectly related to the abuse of human freedom. Without the Fall of man in history, creation would still be perfect (Genesis 1:31). Still, much physical evil is not directly related to human choices. Natural

---

[200]Alvin Plantinga, *God, Freedom, and Evil* (Grand Rapids: William B. Eerdmans Publishing Company, 1974), 28.

[201]Ibid.
[202]Ibid.

[203]Geisler and Corduan, 364.

disasters such as earthquakes, floods, hurricanes, and deaths of innocent infants are examples of physical evil.

Geisler and Corduan list five explanations for physical evil.[204] None of the five are meant to be all-encompassing. Each explains some of the physical evil that occurs. First, some physical evil is necessary for moral perfection.[205] There can be no courage without something evil to fear. Misery is needed for there to be sympathy. Tribulation is needed for there to be endurance and patience.[206] For God to build these characteristics in man, He must permit a certain amount of physical evil.

Second, human free choices do cause some physical evil.[207] It would be an obvious error to assume that no physical evil is caused by the abuse of human free will. The choice to drink and drive has caused much physical evil. Many infants have been born with an addiction to cocaine due to their mothers' choice to abuse drugs while pregnant. It is impossible for God to remove all physical evil without tampering with human free will.[208] It is even possible that some major natural disasters are caused by the evil choices of humans. According to the Bible, this was the case with Sodom and Gomorrah (Genesis 18:20-21; 19).

Third, some physical evil is caused by the choices of demons.[209] The Scriptures speak of demons (fallen angels led by Satan) causing suffering to humans (Job 1, 2; Mark 5:1-20). Demons oppose God and His plans, but they will ultimately be defeated by Christ (Rev. 19, 20, 21, 22).

---

[204]Ibid., 372-378.

[205]Ibid., 372-373.

[206]Ibid., 372.

[207]Ibid., 373.

[208]Ibid., 373-374.

[209]Ibid., 375.

Fourth, God often uses physical evil as a moral warning.[210] Physical pain is often a warning that greater suffering will follow if behavior is not changed. Examples of this would be excessive coughing that is often caused by smoking and heavy breathing caused by over training during a physical workout. Also, God may use pain and suffering to cause a person to focus on Him, rather than on worldly pleasures.[211]

Fifth, some physical evils are necessary in the present state of the physical world.[212] To survive, animals often eat other animals. Humans eat animals as well. It appears that, at least in the present state of the creation, lower life forms are subjected to pain and death in order to facilitate the preservation of higher life forms.[213]

Physical evil, therefore, does not present insurmountable problems for Christian theism. Though man is limited in knowledge and cannot infallibly ascertain why God allows each and every case of physical evil, the five reasons given above should suffice to show that the presence of physical evil in no way rules out the existence of the God of the Bible.

Once the Christian has provided strong evidence for God's existence, he need only give possible reasons why an all-good and all-powerful God would allow evil and human suffering. God has good reasons for allowing evil and human suffering, even though we may not know them fully. Therefore, the existence of evil does not disprove the existence of an all-good and all-powerful God. These two are not mutually exclusive.

The evidence is clear. Atheists have failed to disprove the existence of God, and a strong case can be made that a personal, creator God does exist. However, a person should not be content with embracing God's existence. Each person should examine the centuries of human history to see if this one true God has revealed Himself to man.

---

[210]Ibid., 376.

[211]Ibid.

[212]Ibid.

[213]Ibid., 376-378.

SUGGESTED READING

Books Defending Belief in God:

Dembski, William and Sean McDowell. *Understanding Intelligent Design*. Eugene: Harvest House Publishers, 2008.

D'Souza, Dinesh. *What's So Great About Christianity*. Washington, DC: Regnery Press, Inc., 2007.

Flew, Antony. *There is a God: How the World's Most Notorious Atheist Changed His Mind*. New York: Harper Collins, 2007.

Geisler, Norman L. *Twelve Points that Show Christianity is True*. Indian Trail, North Carolina: NGIM, 2016.

Geisler, Norman L. and Frank Turek. *I Don't Have Enough Faith to Be an Atheist*. Wheaton: Crossway Books, 2004.

Habermas, Gary R. "The Plight of the New Atheism: A Critique" *Journal of the Evangelical Theological Society*. Volume 51, No. 4, December, 2008. pp.813-   827.

Hahn, Scott and Benjamin Wiker. *Answering the New Atheism*. Steubenville, Ohio: Emmaus Road Publishing, 2008.

Lennox, John C. *God's Undertaker: Has Science Buried God?* Oxford: Lion Hudson, 2007.

Books on Debates between Theists and Atheists:

Fernandes, Phil and Michael Martin. *Theism vs. Atheism: The Internet Debate*. Bremerton, WA: IBD Press, 2000.

Hitchens, Christopher and Douglas Wilson. *Is Christianity Good for the World?* Moscow, ID: Canon Press, 2008.

Moreland, J. P. and Kai Nielsen. *Does God Exist? The Great Debate*. Nashville: Thomas   Nelson Publishers, 1990.

Stewart, Robert B. ed. *The Future of Atheism: Alister McGrath and Daniel Dennett in Dialogue*. Minneapolis: Fortress Press, 2008.